My New Book of Words 2

Nina Gontar

Queensland

T0360373

Name: _____

My New Book of Words 2: Queensland

Text: Nina Gontar
Illustrations: Nina Gontar
Editor: Jarrah Moore
Designer: Karen Mayo
Production controller: Renee Cusmano

Acknowledgements
Dedicated to Vanessa, a true friend.

Text © 2012 Nina Gontar
Illustrations © 2012 Nina Gontar

ISBN 978 0 17 019524 9

Cengage Learning Australia
Level 7, 80 Dorcas Street
South Melbourne, Victoria Australia 3205
Phone: 1300 790 853

Cengage Learning New Zealand
Unit 4B Rosedale Office Park
331 Rosedale Road, Albany, North Shore NZ 0632
Phone: 0800 449 725

For learning solutions, visit **cengage.com.au**

Printed in China by RR Donnelley Asia Printing Solutions Limited
1 2 3 4 5 6 7 16 15 14 13 12

Contents

Building Sounds

ang s**ang**	**ing** th**ing**	**ong** s**ong**	**ung** fl**ung**

ack bl**ack**	**eck** n**eck**	**ick** st**ick**	**ock** cl**ock**	**uck** d**uck**

all b**all**	**ell** f**ell**ow	**ill** s**ill**y	**oll** f**oll**ow	**ull** p**ull**

sh **sh**ut	**th** **th**ank	**ch** **ch**icken	**wh** **wh**en	**tch** di**tch**

A	**ai** tr**ai**n	**ay** st**ay**	**a_e** c**a**k**e**	**a** **a**ngel

E	**ee** f**ee**ds	**ea** t**ea**cher	**e_e** th**e**m**e**	**e** sh**e**

I	**igh** n**igh**t	**y** fl**y**	**i_e** **i**nsid**e**	**i** Fr**i**day

O	**oa** b**oa**t	**ow** sh**ow**	**o_e** h**o**m**e**	**o** g**o**

U	**ew** n**ew**	**oo** b**oo**t	**u_e** fl**u**t**e**	**u** m**u**sic

Add **s** star**s**	Add **es** bush**es**	Add **ed** talk**ed**	Add **ly** quick**ly**	Add **est** loud**est**	Add **ing** talk**ing**

ou ho**u**se

ow br**ow**n

ar b**ar**ked

a m**a**sk

eer d**eer**

ear h**ear**

oy b**oy**

oi c**oi**n

ea h**ea**d

ie fr**ie**ndly

a m**a**ny

air h**air**y

ear w**ear**

are sh**are**

ere th**ere**

ir f**ir**st

er h**er**

ur t**ur**n

or w**or**ld

ore m**ore**

aw cr**aw**l

our f**our**

oor d**oor**

oar r**oar**

5

Annoying amphibians make alligators angry.

above		Adelaide
across		Antarctica
aeroplane		Anzac Day
after		Arctic Ocean
afternoon		
again		
almost		
also		
animal		
another		
answer		
anything		
around		
asked		
asleep		
ate		
away		

b   **B**

Bashful brown bears like to hide behind balloons.

beautiful			Bathurst
because			Bondi Beach
began			Brisbane
behind			Broken Hill
believe			
beneath			
beside			
between			
bicycle			
blind			
born			
bought			
boyfriend			
breakfast			
brought			
build			
buy			

Clowns climb with care onto colourful cans.

called	celery
came	cents
carried	circle
castle	circus
caught	city
clean	
close	
clothes	
coming	
computer	
contact	
corner	
could	
cousin	
crawl	
cried	
cry	

Canada
Capricorn
Celsius
Chinese
    New Year

d   D

Don't disturb dogs when they're dancing to hip-hop.

dangerous

date

dear

decided

dictionary

different

digital

dirty

disappear

dodge

does

done

drain

dream

drink

drive

drought

Denmark

DNA

Dreamtime

Dubbo

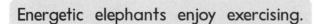

Energetic elephants enjoy exercising.

each

early

eat

edge

either

email

enormous

enough

environment

even

every

everybody

everyone

everything

everywhere

exciting

explain

Earth

East Timor

Egypt

Ethiopia

A fairy's favourite food is fairy floss.

faced
family
farmed
fast
favourite
few
finally
find
finish
first
for
found
friend
frighten
front
full
funny

February
Fiji
France
Fremantle

Gigantic gorillas like to graze on green grass.

game

garage

gave

getting

girlfriend

given

glasses

glitter

glue

goes

gone

good

goodbye

great

group

grow

guess

Galaxy

Great Barrier Reef

Greece

Guatemala

Horses in hats hold their heads up high.

hair
happened
happily
happy
hard
have
having
head
heard
heavy
height
here
hero
holiday
how
hungry
hurtful

Haiti
Halloween
Hawaii
Hong Kong

Interesting insects are everywhere!

ice	
ignore	
imagination	
imagine	
important	
include	
incorrect	
insect	
inside	
instant	
instead	
interesting	
invisible	
invitation	
issue	
itchy	
itself	

ice-cream

idea

idol

iron

island

I'd

India

Internet

Italy

Joeys in jackets just jump and jump and jump.

jacket			Jakarta
jaw			Jamaica
jealous			Japan
jeans			Jupiter
jeer			
jellyfish			
jewellery			
join			
joke			
journal			
journey			
judge			
juice			
juicy			
jumped			
jungle			
just			

k   **K**

Do kind kangaroos like to kiss cute koalas?

keen	knew	Katoomba
keenly	knit	Kenya
keep	knock	Korea
kept	know	Kuwait
key	knowledge	
kicking		
kill		
kilt		
kind		
kindergarten		
kindness		
kingdom		
kissed		
kit		
kitchen		
kite		
kitten		

Large lions laugh at little lions licking lollipops.

lady
large
last
lately
laugh
learnt
leave
letter
light
likely
listen
lived
loose
lose
loud
love
lucky

Launceston
Leo
Libra
Libya

Mischievous mermaids cause magical mix-ups.

machine		Miss
made		Mr
magic		Mrs
make		Ms
making		
many		
measure		
message		
might		
mistake		
money		
more		
morning		
most		
mother		
much		
myself		

n **N**

Never number noodles!

*n*ame
*n*arrow
*n*ear
*n*eed
*n*est
*n*ever
*n*ew
*n*ext
*n*ice
*n*ight
*n*o
*n*obody
*n*one
*n*ose
*n*othing
*n*ow
*n*owhere

New Zealand
North Pole
November
Nullarbor Plain

Oscar the octopus only eats oranges.

oblong		Oceania
ocean		October
offer		Olympics
often		Orion
once		
only		
open		
opposite		
or		
other		
otherwise		
our		
ourselves		
outside		
over		
owe		
own		

Parrots, pigs and pelicans make perfect pets for pirates.

parents
party
past
pencil
people
picture
piece
place
playground
please
pool
present
printer
probably
pull
push
put

Paris
Peru
Pisces
Pluto

The quiet queen quite enjoys a quick game of quoits.

qualify			Quebec
quality			Queensland
quantity			Queenstown
quarrel			
quarter			
queen			
question			
queue			
quick			
quickest			
quiet			
quietly			
quilt			
quit			
quite			
quiz			
quote			

Rollerblading rabbits race faster than robots.

*r*abbit		Romania
*r*are		Rugby League
*r*ather		Rugby Union
*r*eady		Russia
*r*eally		
*r*eceive		
*r*ectangle		
*r*emember		
*r*escue		
*r*eturn		
*r*hyme		
*r*ight		
*r*oll		
*r*oom		
*r*ough		
*r*ound		
*r*ush		

Slithering snakes hiss when sausages sizzle.

said
sandwich
save
saw
scary
school
sentence
should
show
sister
skid
slide
someone
something
sometimes
stayed
suddenly

Saturn
South Australia
South Pole
Sydney

Tiny tortoises are trying to trap a tarantula.

take
taste
telephone
television
thank
their
there
these
they
thought
through
together
told
tomorrow
tonight
tried
turn

Tasman Sea
Taurus
Tokyo
Townsville

Umbrellas go up, and we go under!

ugly
umpire
unable
uncomfortable
underneath
understand
undo
uniform
unit
unless
until
upon
upset
upstairs
use
useful
usual

Uganda
Ukraine
Uranus
Uruguay

V **V**

Vegetables in vases look very peculiar.

*v*acation		Venus
*v*alley		Victoria
*v*aluable		Viking
*v*arious		Virgo
*v*erb		
*v*egetable		
*v*ehicle		
*v*ertical		
*v*eterinarian		
*v*ideo		
*v*iew		
*v*iolin		
*v*isit		
*v*isitor		
*v*oice		
*v*olcano		
*v*ote		

W   **W**

Why would a walrus wash a whale with a washcloth?

*w*alk			*Wagga Wagga*
*w*ant			*Wales*
*w*arm			*Wednesday*
*w*as			*Wellington*
*w*atch			
*w*ater			
*w*ear			
*w*eather			
*w*eekend			
*w*ere			
*w*ithout			
*w*oke			
*w*oman			
*w*on			
*w*onderful			
*w*ork			
*w*ould			

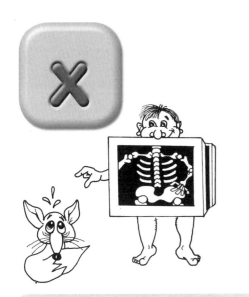

axed   X-ray
exit   xylophone
fixing
pixel
pixie
sixth
sixty

X-ray the fox next, please.

yacht
yard
year
yesterday
yoghurt
you
your

Your yoyo broke
the yellow vase.

zebra
zero
zigzag
zone
zoo
zoom
zucchini

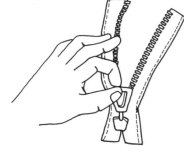

Zip up the zipper!

Abbreviations

N	north	ASAP	as soon as possible	BCE	before Common Era	
S	south	DOB	date of birth	CE	Common Era	
E	east	ETA	estimated time			
W	west		of arrival	Dr	Doctor	
		PTO	Please turn over.	jr	junior	
Ave	Avenue	RSVP	Please reply.	MP	Member of	
Blvd	Boulevard				Parliament	
Dr.	Drive	etc.	and so on	PM	Prime Minister	
St	Street	e.g.	for example	Prof.	Professor	
Rd	Road	i.e.	that is	rep.	representative	
		no.	number	sr	senior	

Actions

abuse	dance	ignite	paddle	tackle
accept	destroy	ignore	poke	talk
admire	drive	imagine	pretend	tidy
bathe	fetch	laugh	raid	uncover
bite	fight	leap	rejoice	undo
build	follow	lunge	relax	unfold
capture	gallop	march	scare	watch
climb	grasp	mend	search	whisper
cuddle	grumble	move	shake	wreck

Add an Ending

word	-er	-est	-ly
dense	denser	densest	densely
fierce	fiercer	fiercest	fiercely
funny	funnier	funniest	funnily
happy	happier	happiest	happily
loud	louder	loudest	loudly
merry	merrier	merriest	merrily
pretty	prettier	prettiest	prettily
smooth	smoother	smoothest	smoothly
warm	warmer	warmest	warmly

Can you think of some more?

 # Sounds

 ai

bait	grain
claim	hail
fail	tail
frail	wait

snails

_____

_____

_____

 ay

always	play
clay	relay
hay	stay
Monday	yesterday

birthday

_____

_____

_____

 a_e

ate	plate
cake	same
crane	shame
late	tame

snakes

_____

_____

_____

a

able	lady
baby	radio
capable	staples
fable	table

labels

_____

_____

_____

32

Better Words

big	little	nice	said	went
colossal	insignificant	courteous	answered	crawled
enlarged	miniature	delicious	asked	dawdled
enormous	minor	delightful	called	jogged
giant	petite	enjoyable	explained	moved
gigantic	short	friendly	mentioned	proceeded
huge	slight	kind	mumbled	raced
immense	small	pleasant	murmured	ran
large	teeny	polite	replied	tiptoed
massive	tiny	tasty	shouted	walked
vast	young	wonderful	whispered	wandered

Birds

bellbird	eagle	lorikeet	quail	swallow
bowerbird	emu	lyrebird	robin	thrush
brolga	finch	magpie	sparrow	wagtail
canary	galah	nightingale	stork	wren
cockatoo	heron	owl		
crane	jay	parrot		
crow	kingfisher	peacock		
dove	kiwi	pelican		
duck	kookaburra	pigeon		

ch Sounds

ch

bea**ch**es	crun**ch**
chain	mar**ch**
chalk	pea**ch**
champion	rea**ch**es
cheat	spee**ch**
choose	tea**ch**er

cheese

tch

ba**tch**	ma**tch**stick
ca**tch**er	pa**tch**
cru**tch**es	pi**tch**er
di**tch**	sti**tch**
ha**tch**ing	stre**tch**
ma**tch**	wa**tch**

witch

t

ac**t**ually	frac**t**ure
adven**t**ure	fu**t**ure
cap**t**ure	mix**t**ure
cen**t**ury	na**t**ure
crea**t**ure	pic**t**ure
even**t**ually	tempera**t**ure

stat**ue**

Compound Words

after + noon = _____

any + one = _____

birth + day = _____

candle + light = _____

grand + child = _____

grand + father = _____

grand + mother = _____

home + work = _____

human + kind = _____

jelly + fish = _____

lip + stick = _____

neck + lace = _____

out + side = _____

play + ground = _____

pop + corn = _____

rain + coat = _____

sand + castle = _____

some + body = _____

some + one = _____

tooth + brush = _____

water + fall = _____

candlelight

35

Computers

address
back up
bit
blog
broadband
byte
cancel
CD-ROM
cell
chatting
Command key
connection
cursor

database
desktop
disk
disk drive
document
dot com
download
file
firewall
gigabyte
hard drive
hardware
home page
icon

ink cartridge
install
Internet
keyboard
laptop
megabyte
memory stick
menu bar
modem
mousepad
network
printer
program

RAM
ROM
scanner
scroll
search
server
shortcut
software
space bar
tab
typing
USB port
virus
website

Email

account
attachment
calendar
contact list
communication
delete

directory
draft
events
folders
junk
log in

mail
message
open
password
receive
send

settings
signature
spam
storage
webmail
write

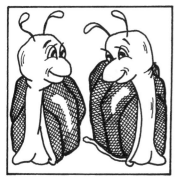

Contractions

Join two words to make a contraction, and don't forget the **apostrophe**.

could have	could've	they are	they're
could not	couldn't	they had	they'd
does not	doesn't	they have	they've
do not	don't	they will	they'll
had not	hadn't	we are	we're
he has	he's	we had	we'd
he is	he's	we have	we've
he will	he'll	we will	we'll
he would	he'd	we would	we'd
I am	I'm	were not	weren't
I have	I've	what is	what's
I will	I'll	where is	where's
I would	I'd	who has	who's
must not	mustn't	who is	who's
she has	she's	who would	who'd
she is	she's	will not	won't
she will	she'll	would not	wouldn't
she would	she'd	you have	you've
there is	there's	you will	you'll
there will	there'll	you would	you'd

 **Sounds**

feet

ee

between	keeping
deepest	meeting
feeling	seen
greenest	wheel

seals

ea

beach	reading
each	reason
neatly	seaside
please	teaching

recycle

e

be	recent
being	remix
detour	she
he	we

e_e

athlete	scene
concrete	supreme
delete	theme
extreme	these

compete

Exercise

aerobics

archery

athletics

ballet

ballroom dancing

baseball

basketball

BMX racing

canoeing

car racing

cricket

cycling

fishing

football

gymnastics

hang-gliding

hockey

horseriding

jogging

judo

karate

kayaking

mountaineering

netball

parachuting

polo

rockclimbing

rollerblading

rowing

sailing

skating

skiing

snowboarding

soccer

softball

squash

surfing

swimming

tenpin bowling

volleyball

walking

water polo

weightlifting

wrestling

 **Sounds**

ph

alphabet	phrase	dolphin
graph	physical	
pamphlet	saxophone	
phone	sphere	
photocopy	triumph	
photograph	trophy	

gh

cough	rough	laugh
coughed	rougher	
coughing	roughly	
enough	tough	
laughing	tougher	
laughter	toughest	

ff

buffalo	fluffy	
cuff	graffiti	
different	puffy	sniffing
difficult	scruffy	
effect	toffee	
fluff	traffic	

Family	Friends	Favourite Food
_____	_____	_____
_____	_____	_____
_____	_____	_____
_____	_____	_____
_____	_____	_____
_____	_____	_____
_____	_____	_____
_____	_____	_____
_____	_____	_____
_____	_____	_____

Fantasy

Once upon a time ...

adventure
alien
battle
defend
dream
enchantress
fairytale
galaxy
giant
goblin
hero
heroine
imagination
legend
magic

magical
make believe
mermaid
monster
myth
prince
princess
protect
robot
space
superhero
unicorn
vampire
villain
wizard

castle

dragon

... happily ever after.

leprechaun

knight

42

Feelings

Angry

annoyed
bitter
cross
enraged
fiery
furious
mad

Happy

cheerful
delighted
glad
jolly
joyful
overjoyed
thrilled

Sad

distressed
downcast
gloomy
glum
sorrowful
troubled
upset

Concerned

alarmed
anxious
bothered
nervous
troubled
uneasy
worried

Impatient

eager
excited
hasty
hurried
impetuous
irritated
keen

Scared

afraid
fearful
frightened
panicky
petrified
startled
terrified

Embarrassed

ashamed
awkward
humiliated
mortified
self-conscious
tongue-tied
uncomfortable

Proud

complacent
conceited
content
pleased
satisfied
smug
vain

Surprised

amazed
astonished
astounded
flabbergasted
shocked
startled
stunned

Fractions

A fraction is what you get when you divide something into smaller equal parts.

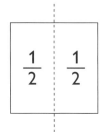

$\frac{1}{2}$ = one-half

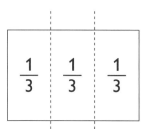

$\frac{1}{3}$ = one-third

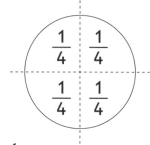

$\frac{1}{4}$ = one-quarter

A fraction is written as two numbers, one above and one below the line.

$$\frac{1}{4}$$

← This number is the **numerator**.

← This number is the **denominator**.

The numerator tells you how many parts there are.
The denominator tells you how many parts you would need to make a whole.

$\frac{1}{4}$ = one-quarter

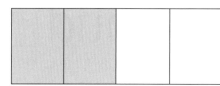

$\frac{2}{4}$ = two-quarters

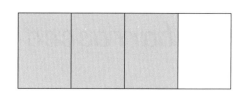

$\frac{3}{4}$ = three-quarters

$\frac{1}{5}$ = one-fifth

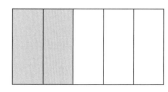

$\frac{2}{5}$ = two-fifths

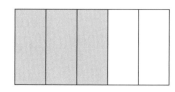

$\frac{3}{5}$ = three-fifths

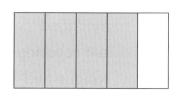

$\frac{4}{5}$ = four-fifths

Government

- [ ] Australian Greens
- [ ] Australian Labor Party
- [ ] Liberal Party of Australia
- [ ] National Party of Australia

Assembly
Cabinet
chairperson
committee

community
Constitution
councillor
democracy
deputy lord mayor
election
governor-general
independent
lord mayor
mayor
minister

Opposition
Parliament
party
politician
premier
prime minister
Senate
senator
shire council
treasurer
vote

Grammar

adjective
adverb
clause
collective noun
conjunction
connective
future tense
homophone

noun
paragraph
past tense
phrase
plural
preposition
present tense
pronoun

proper noun
question
sentence
singular
statement
tense
title
verb

Homophones

ate	I **ate** my dinner.	**flour**	I use **flour** to make cakes.
eight	She has **eight** dogs.	**flower**	The **flower** smells lovely.
be	It will **be** sunny today.	**for**	I will go **for** a walk.
bee	A **bee** can sting you.	**four**	Two plus two equals **four**.
berry	I will eat the **berry**.	**hair**	My **hair** is curly.
bury	Dogs **bury** bones.	**hare**	The **hare** can run quickly.
blew	I **blew** lots of bubbles.	**hear**	I can **hear** the song playing.
blue	Is the sky **blue**?	**here**	Come **here**, please.
brake	My bike has a **brake**.	**knew**	I **knew** his name.
break	Did you **break** the cup?	**new**	That toy is **new**.
buy	Go and **buy** an apple.	**knight**	The **knight** sits on a horse.
by	I run **by** myself.	**night**	At **night** I sleep in my bed.
chews	The cow **chews** grass.	**know**	I **know** my age.
choose	**Choose** me, please.	**no**	Yes is the opposite of **no**.
dear	**Dear** Santa …	**knows**	She **knows** her address.
deer	A **deer** has hooves.	**nose**	My **nose** is itchy!
die	Plants **die** without water.	**made**	I **made** my own bed.
dye	I will **dye** my pants red.	**maid**	The **maid** washed the dishes.
eye	My **eye** is sore.	**mail**	I will **mail** the letter.
I	**I** am a happy person.	**male**	A **male** duck is a drake.

meat	Do you eat red **meat**?	**sea**	Fish swim in the **sea**.
meet	**Meet** me at the zoo.	**see**	I can **see** the mountains.
oar	In my boat is an **oar**.	**sew**	I **sew** with a needle.
or	Do you prefer red **or** blue?	**so**	I am **so** hungry.
one	I have **one** nose.	**some**	Would you like **some** fruit?
won	Who **won** the race?	**sum**	One plus one is a **sum**.
pair	I own a **pair** of sneakers.	**son**	Her **son** is a clever boy.
pear	I ate a **pear** at lunchtime.	**sun**	The **sun** is up in the sky.
plain	I like **plain** sandwiches.	**tail**	My dog's **tail** is so long.
plane	The **plane** flew away.	**tale**	A **tale** is a story.
read	I have **read** this book.	**their**	That is **their** car.
red	My apple is **red**.	**there**	Go over **there**!
right	Will you go left or **right**?	**waist**	My belt goes around my **waist**.
write	I love to **write** stories.	**waste**	Don't **waste** water!
road	The **road** was bumpy.	**wear**	I **wear** a school uniform.
rode	I **rode** my horse today.	**where**	**Where** is my dog?
sail	My boat has a white **sail**.	**which**	**Which** hat do you like?
sale	My computer was on **sale**.	**witch**	A **witch** can do magic.
scent	This rose has a **scent**.	**wood**	I put **wood** on the fire.
sent	Mum **sent** me shopping.	**would**	**Would** you like to play?

 **Sounds**

i

bicycle	kindest
blind	mind
child	triangle
find	wild

spiders

_____
_____
_____

i_e

fine	quite
grime	shine
inside	time
pile	write

smiles

_____
_____
_____

igh

bright	might
fight	nightmare
high	right
lightning	tight

night

_____
_____
_____

y

by	shy
dry	sky
fly	try
myself	why

cry

_____
_____
_____

"ie" or "ei"?

Put "i" before "e" ...

achieve	brief	niece	thief
belief	chief	piece	thieves
believe	grief	relief	unbelievable

... except after "c" ...

ceiling	conceive	deceive	receipt
conceit	deceit	inconceivable	receive
conceited	deceitful	perceive	receiving

... when the sound you hear is "ee".
But not when it's "ay", as in "n**ei**ghbour" or "w**ei**gh".

eight	freight	sleigh	vein
eighty	reins	veil	weight

While these words tease and just do as they please!

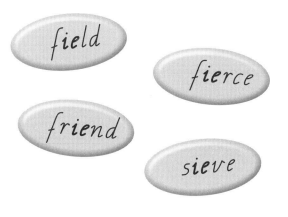

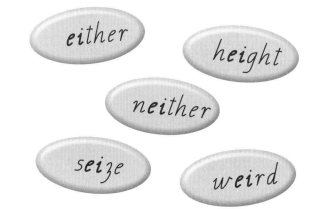

49

Sounds

giraffes

g

engine	germ
gem	giant
general	gigantic
generally	ginger
generous	magic
gentle	magician

ge

oranges

age	language
arrange	large
bandage	page
change	stage
charge	strange
garbage	village

dge

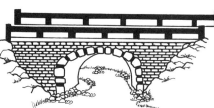

bridge

badge	hedge
dodge	judge
edge	ledge
fidget	porridge
fridge	ridge
gadget	wedge

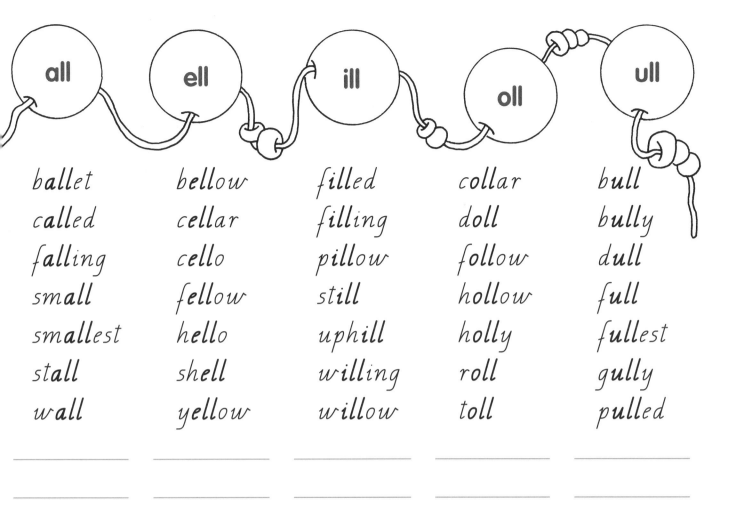

all	ell	ill	oll	ull
ballet	bellow	filled	collar	bull
called	cellar	filling	doll	bully
falling	cello	pillow	follow	dull
small	fellow	still	hollow	full
smallest	hello	uphill	holly	fullest
stall	shell	willing	roll	gully
wall	yellow	willow	toll	pulled

Liquids

apple cider	cream	lemonade	sauce
bleach	custard	milk	shampoo
blood	detergent	milkshake	soft drink
brake fluid	fruit juice	mineral water	soup
broth	fruit punch	nail polish	soy sauce
bubble bath	ginger beer	oil	tea
coffee	green tea	paint	tears
conditioner	handwash	perfume	vinegar
cordial	honey	petrol	water

Maths

10	ten
20	twenty
30	thirty
40	forty
50	fifty
60	sixty
70	seventy
80	eighty
90	ninety
100	one hundred
1000	one thousand
1000 000	one million

Abbreviations

C	Celsius	**km**	kilometre	**mL**	millilitre
cm	centimetre	**L**	litre	**mm**	millimetre
g	gram	**m**	metre	**sec.**	second
hr	hour	**mg**	milligram	**vol.**	volume
kg	kilogram	**min.**	minute		

Vocabulary

add	fraction	radius
amount	graph	scales
angle	height	solid
area	horizontal	square
calculator	length	subtract
cents	line	temperature
circumference	measure	thermometer
cube	multiply	time
decimal	number	vertical
diameter	ordinal	volume
divide	pair	weigh
dollars	parallel	weight
equal	percentage	whole
estimate	perimeter	width

oa Sounds

o

go	no
going	ochre
gross	only
most	so

post

boat

oa

boast	goal
coat	goat
float	roast
foal	toast

rope

o_e

alone	note
cone	phone
home	stone
hope	vote

bows

ow

crow	low
flow	mow
grow	row
know	show

53

Other Sounds

Put the book down.

U

bull	fullest
bullied	pull
bush	pulled
full	push

oo

cook	looked
footpath	shook
good	stood
hood	took

The cow is outside.

ow

clown	now
down	power
growled	towel
how	wow

ou

about	loudly
cloud	our
counting	round
found	sound

The toy robot is noisy.

oy

annoy	joy
boy	joyful
destroy	oyster
enjoy	royal

oi

avoid	point
choice	poison
disappoint	toilet
noise	voice

This is the last **jar**.

 a

ask	h**a**lf
br**a**ss	m**a**sk
f**a**st	p**a**ss
gr**a**ssy	p**a**st

 ar

b**ar**ked	c**ar**ve
b**ar**n	d**ar**ling
c**ar**pet	sn**ar**l
c**ar**toon	st**ar**ve

A **deer** app**ear**ed.

 eer

ch**eer**	sh**eer**
ch**eer**ful	st**eer**
j**eer**	v**eer**
p**eer**	volunt**eer**

ear

b**ear**d	g**ear**s
cl**ear**	h**ear**
d**ear**	n**ear**ly
f**ear**ed	y**ear**

Careful!
There's a h**air**y b**ear**!

are

b**are**
b**are**ly
c**are**
d**are**
gl**are**
h**are**

ere

anywh**ere**
everywh**ere**
nowh**ere**
th**ere**
th**ere**fore
wh**ere**

air

ch**air**
d**air**y
f**air**
f**air**y
p**air**
st**air**s

ear

b**ear**
p**ear**
sw**ear**
t**ear**
t**ear**ing
w**ear**

Places to Visit

aquarium	Australian War Memorial	Lord Howe Island
art gallery	Blue Mountains	Luna Park
beach	Centennial Park	Murray River
botanical garden	Coober Pedy	Nullarbor Plain
lighthouse	Darling Harbour	Sydney Harbour Bridge
museum	Gold Coast	Tasmanian Wilderness
outback	Great Barrier Reef	Taronga Zoo
rainforest	Kakadu National Park	Three Sisters
theatre	Kimberley	Twelve Apostles
theme park	Lake Eyre	Uluru

People to Meet

architect	blueprints, bricks, buildings, cement, designs, drawings, plans
artist	brushes, canvas, chalk, charcoal, crayons, easel, paint, palette
baker	apron, baking, biscuits, bread, cakes, dough, flour, oven
chef	bake, boil, bowls, fry, kitchen, pans, recipe, refrigerator, stove
electrician	equipment, extension cord, pliers, tape, toolbox, van, wires
florist	arrangements, bouquets, flowers, fragrance, plants, ribbons
mechanic	engine, grease, oil, overalls, screwdriver, spanner, spark plug
plumber	blocked, dig, drain, excavate, pipes, sink, spade, toilet, water
police officer	accident, bikes, cars, law, offender, protect, station, thief, traffic
reporter	articles, interviews, investigation, magazine, newspaper, stories
writer	books, imagination, manuscript, paper, publish, story, typing

Punctuation Marks

,   *apostrophe*

( )   *brackets*

Brackets go around extra information (like this bit).

●   *bullet point*

:   *colon*

,   *comma*

A comma is a pause in a sentence, like this.

—   *dash*

!   *exclamation mark*

Use an exclamation mark when a sentence is exciting!

.   *full stop*

Put a full stop at the end of a sentence.

?   *question mark*

Where do you put a question mark?

" "   *quotation marks*

/   *slash*

Repeat the Letter

bb abbreviation, babble, bubble, bubblegum, cabbage, chubby, grubby, hobby, nibble, pebble, rabbit, ribbon, rubbish

cc accelerate, accent, accept, acceptable, accessories, accident, accommodate, accompany, broccoli, hiccup, occur, success

dd add, address, cuddle, giddy, hidden, ladder, middle, odd, paddle, paddock, peddle, puddle, riddle, suddenly

ff affect, cliff, coffin, different, difficult, effect, fluffy, muffin, off, offend, offer, office, puff, puffy, ruffian, sniff, stuff, whiff

gg biggest, dagger, digging, eggs, giggle, goggles, jogger, juggle, luggage, smuggle, snuggle, stagger, trigger, wiggle, wriggle

mm clammy, comma, commercial, common, community, dummy, hammer, mammal, simmer, summer, tummy, yummy

nn announce, annoy, antenna, banner, beginning, channel, dinner, goanna, granny, manners, nanny, spanner, tennis, winner

pp appear, appearance, apple, apply, approach, approve, disappear, flippers, happen, happiness, happy, pepper, puppet

ss across, address, bassinet, blossom, boss, chess, class, compass, dessert, fuss, glass, hiss, lesson, miss, mission, pass, toss

tt attempt, better, bitter, clutter, glitter, kettle, kitty, letter, litter, little, mittens, mutter, pattern, rattle, settle, shatter, wattle

Schwa

Uh?

The letters **a**, **e**, **i**, **o**, **u** are called vowels, and they have lots of different sounds. Schwa is the lazy and quiet vowel sound you can hear in many words. Say the words "ago" and "dinner". Can you hear the "uh"? That's the schwa. Schwa sounds like "uh", no matter what vowel it is.

When you write a word with schwa in it, it's easy to get the spelling wrong, because all you can hear is the "uh" sound.

a	e	i	o	u
about	enough	decimal	actor	album
around	monster	easily	complete	bonus
balloon	sister	pencil	gallop	circus
banana	taken	terrible	harmony	picture
umbrella	winner	victim	mosquito	Uluru

Can you think of more words with the schwa sound?

 **Sounds**

 sh

fashion   pushing
friendship   rushed
gushing   shadow
mashed   shutting

fisherman

 c

ancient   malicious
delicious   precious
efficient   suspicious
ferocious   vicious

liquorice

 ss

assure   permission
discussion   possession
expression   pressure
mission   reassure

tissue

 t

action   fraction
correction   multiplication
demolition   relaxation
education   subtraction

addition

Shapes and Objects

2D Shapes

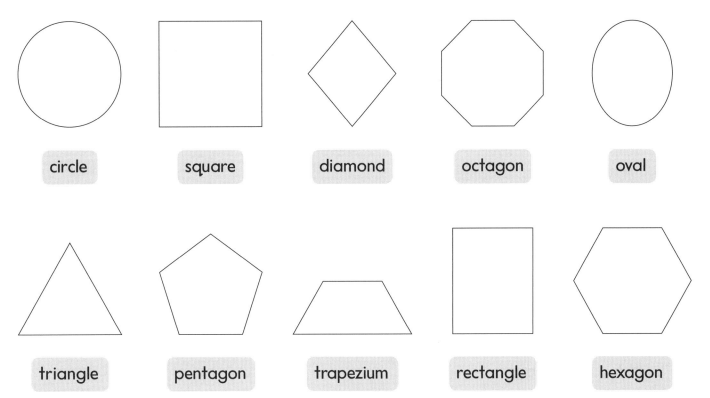

circle

square

diamond

octagon

oval

triangle

pentagon

trapezium

rectangle

hexagon

3D Objects

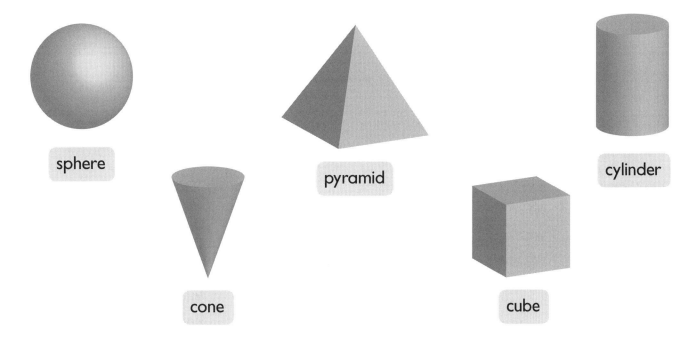

sphere

pyramid

cylinder

cone

cube

Silent Sounds

b
- bom**b**
- clim**b**
- com**b**
- crum**b**
- de**b**t
- dou**b**t
- dum**b**
- num**b**
- plum**b**er
- thum**b**

g
- desi**g**n
- **g**nash
- **g**naw
- **g**nome
- rei**g**n
- resi**g**n
- si**g**n

h
- **gh**ost
- **h**eir
- **h**onour
- **h**our
- w**h**at
- w**h**en
- w**h**ere
- w**h**ether
- w**h**ile
- w**h**ite
- w**h**y

gh
- bri**gh**t
- dau**gh**ter
- hei**gh**t
- hi**gh**
- nei**gh**bour
- ni**gh**t
- si**gh**
- si**gh**t
- sli**gh**t
- strai**gh**t
- tau**gh**t
- thou**gh**t
- wei**gh**

p
- cor**p**s
- cu**p**board
- **p**neumonia
- **p**sychiatrist
- **p**terodactyl
- ras**p**berry
- recei**p**t

t
- balle**t**
- buffe**t**
- cas**t**le
- croche**t**
- debu**t**
- depo**t**
- fas**t**en
- gourme**t**
- this**t**le
- vale**t**
- whis**t**le
- wres**t**ler

w
- answer
- **s**word
- t**w**o
- **w**ho
- **w**hole
- **w**hose
- **w**rap
- **w**reck
- **w**ren
- **w**restle
- **w**rist
- **w**ritten
- **w**rong
- **w**rote

k
- **k**nead
- **k**nee
- **k**new
- **k**nife
- **k**night
- **k**nit
- **k**nitting
- **k**nock
- **k**nuckle

Sounds

ss

acro**ss**	dre**ss**
bo**ss**y	flo**ss**
cla**ss**	le**ss**on
cro**ss**ed	pre**ss**ed

address

_____

_____

_____

_____

se

ca**se**	mou**se**
el**se**	nur**se**
gee**se**	pur**se**
hou**se**	sen**se**

horse

_____

_____

_____

_____

ce

boun**ce**	pea**ce**
dan**ce**	pie**ce**
glan**ce**	pri**ce**
on**ce**	sin**ce**

fence

_____

_____

_____

_____

c

ac**c**ent	**c**ircus
cents	**c**itizen
cinema	**c**ity
circle	**c**ivilisation

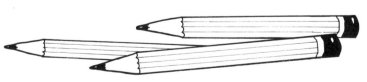

pencils

_____

_____

_____

_____

Technology

Digital Camera

battery	focus	photo	shutter speed
buttons	format	pixel	storage
colours	image	printing	thumbnail
contrast	megapixel	red-eye	transfer
delete	memory card	resolution	upload
flash	mode	sensor	zoom

Video Game

adventure	joystick
audio	level
console	monitor
controller	multiplayer
gamepad	platform
handheld	player
interactive	television

MP3 Player

album	playlist
artist	previous track
audio file	rip
click wheel	scrolling
headphones	shuffle
next track	song
pause	volume

Mobile Phone

accessories	GPS navigation
address book	memo
calculator	ringtone
contact list	smartphone
conversation	text message

E-Reader

battery life	read
bookmark	reader
e-book	screen
format	stylus
novel	text size